Recollections of my Childhood

The true story of a childhood lived in the times of Napoleon Bonaparte

Transcribed from Frances Rainsford's original manuscript by Jane McLellan and published in this form by Julie Garland McLellan.

ISBN-13: 978-1456495060

Copyright © 2010 by Julie Garland McLellan

1st Edition published in 2010 by Great Governance

Foreword

This book has been transcribed from the original manuscript written by the Frances Sophia McLellan neé Rainsford, daughter of Captain Thomas Rainsford and Jane Hannay. She married into the McLellan family and the book was passed down through Frederick John McLellan and his sister Jane F McLellan, then to Andrew John Lines McLellan and then to David Aksel Hannay McLellan; the husband of the publisher. I look forward to passing it down, in turn, to our son Andrew James McLellan.

References have been checked where possible and some inconsistencies between this memoir and historical dates are noted. Most of the events depicted in this memoir are consistent with the historical timeline against which they are set.

This work has been transcribed to share the life story of the protagonist with interested persons, both within her family and beyond, rather than as a serious historical investigation.

Although the aim of this book is to amuse, rather than to educate, as I was reading through the manuscript I could not help but notice the resilience, cheerfulness and spirit of gratitude with which the manuscript is brimming. If the reader can learn, from this book, how to face adverse circumstance with the fortitude displayed by the little girl who penned the original and lived the story, then this book will have made a significant contribution, if not to our understanding of the past, then to our ability to endure the present and construct a better future.

I hope you will enjoy reading it as much as I did.

Julie Garland McLellan

Sydney, Australia, 2010

Contents

Recollections of my childhood 7
    Introduction 7
    France 9
    England 19
    Voyage around the Cape 23
    St Helena 33
    Return to England 41
    England Again 43
    Life Alone 45
    Looking back 49
    Historical Notes 50

Recollections of my Childhood

Introduction

When you were all children and we used to be sitting around the fire in the long winter evenings the chief amusement used to be telling stories and when my stock was exhausted I was often asked to tell what I did when I was a little girl.

The request has been made again, and I shall endeavour to put down what I can remember of a time that was very eventful, but being only a little girl I can give only a childish account of what made a lasting impression upon me.

France

Father was a captain Rainsford Hannay of the guards[1]. His father was a colonel of the guards. As far as I know my father and brother went over to France in 1802[2], taking with them my two eldest brothers and sisters, two servants and my brother's two favourite dogs. What took them there I don't know, but they must have intended remaining there are some time. They had not been long at Amiens till war broke out[3], and they were taken prisoners. They did not remain long at Amiens but were sent to Valenciennes. There a little sister was born, and only lived a very short time. Then they were sent to Verdun, then back to Valenciennes, where I made my appearance on the stage.

---

[1] Probably Captain Thomas Rainsford, of the 2nd Life Guards, Married to Jane Hannay, Daughter of Sir Robert Hannay and Mary Mead.

[2] Many British went to France in 1802 and 1803 during the brief period of peace that followed the signing of the Treaty of Amiens.

[3] Both the British and French violated the Treaty of Amiens and the British Government declared war on France in May 1803.

In a short time back to Verdun again, although the first thing I remember is living in a nice house in the country. The place belonged to two old French ladies. There was a beautiful garden, and orchard, and a green sloping bank with a burn[4] at the foot where the elder ones used to dabble.

The old ladies took great pleasure in their orchard, and the apples were kept in a press or armoire at the end of a long passage, and the first thing I remember was your uncle Bill[5] trotting after the old ladies and his first words were "pommes, pommes", and the old ladies gave him apples.

My father did not sleep there, he came early in the morning, and spent the day, but he was obliged to return to Verdun in the evening. Verdun was very strongly fortified. The 'détenus' were up on their 'pasale' and might not go away they liked during the day. There was a drawbridge, which was always guarded. It was drawn up at sunrise, and let down at sunset. The male prisoners had pass-ports which they left in the guard room when they went to the country, and if they did not return for them by sunset, the

---

[44] 'Burn' is Scottish for stream.

[5] William Henry Hannay was the son of Captain Thomas Rainford and Jane Hannay. He married Maria Dalrymple. He died in 1856, without children.

bridge was let down and they were popped into prison next day.

They were very strictly guarded, but kindly treated, and the French were very fond of the English. Wives and children were allowed to come home, but latterly this leave was withdrawn, as many gentlemen sent their wives and children home, and then escaped in disguise. My brother and sister must have been the last to get leave to come home, and they must have been away about a year, but they left in the summer, and must have returned at the same season. Soon after their return there were great rejoicings at the birth of the little king of Rome in 1812[6], and I still remember sketches and songs composed upon the occasion, particularly two or three lines of one beginning "Napoleon te voila Pére, tes désirs sont tous cumplis".

But though he had got all his wishes, his reign was drawing to a close. I remember his passing through Verdun incognito, in a very plain travelling carriage and pair. My father held me up at the window to see

---

[6] Napoleon married Marie Louise, Archduchess of Austria, in March 1810. The couple had one child, Napoleon Francis Joseph Charles (1811–1832), known from birth as the King of Rome. He became Napoleon II in 1814 and reigned for only two weeks. He died of tuberculosis aged 21, with no children.

him pass. I saw a figure in the carriage, but that was all.

The conscription was a very sad thing, all the young men went to the wars, and there were only old men and children left.

I remember the rations that the prisoners used to get. To each a certain allowance of beef and brown bread, and peas, or beans, for soup. There was a kind of serge given out for underclothing for all ages.

The end of 1813; the winter set in very severely, and the French army suffered greatly during the Russian campaign. I remember the frost was so severe that when we went to play in the garden our fingers used to bleed with the cold. My father used to have the map out constantly to trace the progress of the allies, and they were approaching very near. Then one day at the very beginning of January, it was given out that the prisoners were to march in the course of two days to Blois[7]. What was to be done? Go they must. There was not a vehicle of any kind to be got except a little market cart, which used to bring in butter and eggs etc. to the market. This, Papa was thankful to get for mamma and the children, and on a bitter, cold morning we started on our dreary journey.

---

[7] This is a distance of some 400km.

My father and the elder ones walking, and mamma and the three little ones (myself and two younger brothers), and a large cage containing the birds, in the cart. Poor mamma felt the cold very much, and her hair was hanging in icicles. We did not go more than two or three leagues[8] in our little cart, and were thankful to stop at a little wayside inn, where we were told we could get one room when some officers left it. In the meantime we might go into the kitchen and warm ourselves. There was a large stove, and a number of poor French soldiers sitting around it. They all looked very ill, and one of them who was just recovering from typhus fever took me on his knee and warmed me at the stove. At last we got into the room, where there were two beds, we had some supper; there were 10 of us great and small, some of them lay down before a good fire and all slept soundly except when they were disturbed by the howling of the wolves outside. Next day we started early for Chalons[9] where we got into comfortable quarters, but Mama was so ill and frightened about the children

---

[8] The league was a common unit of measurement throughout western Europe, although its length varied greatly from region to region. It was originally intended to represent the distance a person could walk in an hour. In many cases it was equal to 3 miles, (note that the definition of a mile also varied from region to region).

[9] Most likely this was Chalons Sur Marne

that we stayed there for two days and got a fine large comfortable wagon with plenty of hay and opened partly.

So we started quite comfortably and did not feel the cold quite so much though it was freezing quite as hard. The roads were very bad, in fact no roads, merely a way through the fields covered with snow.

One night in particular I remember we were out very late and although we passed through two or three small villages every inn was occupied. At last my father went to the Waggoner and got billets for us in two very poor houses. The people were very kind and did what they could for us, made up a roaring fire of wood and then put on some soup for our supper. We all sat round the fire, and the old woman of the house commenced her cooking operations. First she melted some butter in a large frying pan, then she sliced in some onions, next put in some water and then slices of dark brown bread (almost black) they all got boiled and some seasoning of salt and pepper, a famous supper it made, and we all enjoyed it, being very hungry.

After supper we had to separate, but some of us had to go to our bedroom, which contained two beds, one of which was occupied by my mother and two of the children, and the other by nurse and two more of us.

It was a very cold and miserable place, with an earthen floor, very little fire, and a hole at the bottom of the door for the cat to go in and out. The snow and the wind came blowing in: but the old witchlike woman did her best to make us comfortable, locked us in when she went away.

Next morning we were off again in snow and frost.

Another night I remember very well. There was the same difficulty in getting shelter for the night; at last we got a very small room with one bed and a shakedown. It was next to a larger room where a number of French soldiers were sitting around the stove smoking and drinking. They were very polite and asked us to warm ourselves at the stove, and some of them offered to give up their beds, but mamma preferred getting into the little room with the nurse and my sisters and the children. She was very tired and ill that night, but fortunately we were drawing near to Orleans. The next night we slept there at a comfortable hotel in the Place Dame where there was a fine bronze statue of the Maid of Orleans in full armour. We had to stay at Orleans for some days as poor Mamma was so ill she could not go on, and she's used to amuse herself by copying little drawings of the Maid of Orleans with which the room was hung.

As soon as she was able to move we went to Blois which we must have reached in two days.

When we arrived there was difficulty in getting a house but a comfortable one was soon got. But mamma was very ill all the time we were there. She had a dreadful cough; she got better, but had never been out of the house when the next arrived, and we had to leave Blois for Gleary[10] at the point of the bayonet. Soldiers with drawn swords were stationed in different places to see the prisoners off.

Fortunately we got covered things, buggies they were called, and we got on quicker in these sort of geeks. The weather continued very cold and often they used to meet poor soldiers with their hands and feet frostbitten. At last we got to Gleary – a poor little out-of-the way place with scarcely a decent house in it, but we got a wonderfully good one with a large yard and nice garden. After we had been there about a month the snow began to melt, and there was a slight appearance of spring.

I used to like going out in the morning with my father, and how well I remember when the broom began to show its green leaves, the smell I have never

---

[10] The name is consistently spelt in the manuscript but does not feature on modern maps. It may be Gleize or Glisy.

forgotten. I never see the early broom without thinking of those morning walks with dear papa.

At last, when spring was fairly well set in, early in April, one morning Papa came in quietly excited, and said that news had come that Napoleon had abdicated[11], that the prisoners were all released, and might go where they liked. My Father was greatly rejoiced, but poor Mama looked sad, she knew that a change had taken place in everybody, and everything since she was last in England.

In a few days all the arrangements were made, and we were on the road to Paris, on our way home.

The white Cockade was mounted by everybody and shouts of 'Vive Louis dix-huit!' were heard in all directions.

I don't remember anything about our journey to Paris, except meeting the Cossacks on horseback with their long spears, and being afraid of them.

Paris was very crowded, all the allied sovereigns of Europe being there[12]. I remember seeing the

---

[11] Napoleon abdicated on 6th April 1814.
[12] The Treaty of Fontainebleau was established in Fontainebleau (near Paris) on 11 April 1814 between Napoleon Bonaparte and representatives from Austria, Hungary, Bohemia, Russia, and Prussia.

illuminations, which must have been very grand. Paris must have been a very different place then to what it is now; the streets narrow and not flagged at the sides, but I was too young to remember much about it, except the Jardin des Plantes, and the museum with which I was much delighted. We stayed there about a fortnight, and then went on to Calais, where we remained for a few days, my little brother being ill.

There I first saw the sea. My Father took me to walk on the sands and I was charmed with the small corals and shells and the fisherwomen. He pointed out to me where England was.

England

There were no steamers in those days – nothing but miserable packets. We scarcely lost sight of land but we had a long rough passage, and arrived very sick and wretched at Dover. Everything looked so dreary there and most of us wished ourselves back in France. My little brother exclaiming 'Is this England? Oh! Take me back to France!'

He was soon much pleased with the beautiful horses in the stage coach. We went at a tremendous pace to London, and stopped at an old fashioned inn where many of the coaches put up. It was the 'Spread Eagle' in Grace Church[13]. It was one of the oldest hotels in London and I saw not long ago that it had been pulled down.

The rooms were built around a courtyard with verandas so we could run about and watch the coaches come in. We did not stay there above two or three days till a lodging was got. All Mama's relations had left town and gone to their country places.

---

[13] This was a popular coach house and paintings from the period depict that it was constructed as described.

We found it very dull in a pokey lodging without any garden, and whenever we went out we were hated on account of our dress – the high-crowned bonnets and short waists showing at once that we were French. We were obliged to take a hacking coach, which was rather expensive in those days when money was scarce.

The next lodging we went to was in the Edgeware Road, which was then quite in the country – there were houses on one side with very small gardens in front, and on the opposite side fields and stackyards.

The allied sovereigns by this time had come to London[14], and there were great rejoicings there, grand illuminations among other things, and a sham fight on the Serpentine in Hyde Park.

After my Father had been a short time in London he went to one of the Duke of York's Laics[15]. His Royal Highness remembered him very well and asked him where he had been for so long, and upon hearing that he had been a prisoner of war for seven years, he said

---

[14] The Allied sovereigns' visit to England occurred in June 1814 to celebrate the peace following the defeat of France and abdication of Napoleon Bonaparte in April 1814.

[15] A Laic is a religious function or event involving people who are not ordained clergy.

he would be happy to help him when he had something he could offer him.

Not long afterwards he was informed that he had got a very good appointment out at St. Helena.

Mama was then getting into bad health caused by the hardships she had gone through and felt quite unfit for the long voyage so the appointment was kept open until she should be able to go. But alas! She always got worse, and although she had the best advice London could afford, nothing could be done for her. One day, hearing a conversation between her and one of the doctors, I got very frightened about her, and used to watch her, and gradually I saw a change in her face, and her beautiful hands got thinner and thinner. Winter came on, and her cough got worse and worse, and at last she was confined to bed. We were then living at Brompton and two old ladies, relations of her own, used to come every evening, and they took it in turns to sit up with her.

One night when she seemed worse than usual they sent me off to bed, and I shall never forget how she followed me with her eyes as I left the room, and gave me her last blessing. When leaving the room I heard the doctor say that he thought she could not last the night out.

I went to bed and cried myself to sleep. Next morning early, my father stood beside the bed. I knew at once what had happened – that I had no Mama now. He tried to comfort me and said I should be his little girl.

We all assembled in the room and a dear relation took me by the hand to show me my Mama who was gone to heaven, but I could not look at her and I never saw her again. I saw the coffin that contained all that was so dear to me, but even that in a few days was taken away and we were left alone.

Voyage around the Cape

After the death of dear Mama there was no longer any reason why we should not go to St. Helena, and preparations were made for our departure. The outfit took up our attention but never was dear Mama forgotten, and though I left I never forgot her. I am an old woman now; I remember her as fondly as ever.

The ship we were to go out in sailed from Gravesend, and there we went early in July to be in readiness. When we went on board the 'Princess Charlotte' – for that was the name of the transport[16] – we found everything as wretched as could be. She was crowded

---

[16] There are three possible ships named HMS Princess Charlotte that could have been the one mentioned in the manuscript. One was a 32-gun fifth rate, previously the French ship Junon. She was captured in 1799 and renamed Andromache in 1812. She was broken up in 1828. Another was a schooner listed as being in service between 1805 and 1806. And finally there was a 42-gun fifth rate, originally to have been named HMS Vittoria. She was launched in 1814, was renamed HMS Burlington in 1814 and was sold for breaking up in 1833.

with all sorts of people, some troops (the 92nd Highlanders), a number of officers belonging to different regiments, officers of the Royal Engineers and Artillery, several belonging to the civil service, some bound for the Cape and some going to Ceylon.

There was little time to get our cabin in order for it began to blow as soon as we got into the Channel and we were all very sick and unable to move. We had two cats shut up in a basket, and soon they began to mew, and made their escape and there was a rushing about after them.

It was so stormy that the sea came rushing through the portholes and our miserable little berths were soon wet through, and everything that was not secured was floating about our little cabins. It was so bad that the portholes had to be closed and the only light we had was admitted by the bulbic eyes, so when anybody on deck happened to step upon them, or a sail got on them, we were thrown into total darkness. All this misery lasted till we got out of the Bay of Biscay.

After that we were able to sit up on deck, and some worked or read, and we children were able to play.

The sailors were very good to the boys and the gentlemen on board took a great deal of notice of the little girls. It was an amusement watching the moving of the log, and the various performances of the sailors.

At last, when we had been on board about three weeks and were accustomed to the life, my Father told us one evening that Madeira was to be seen from the mast head and that we should be there next morning.

Accordingly, next morning early he came to our cabin and told us to look out of the porthole, and there we were, close to Funchal.

There was the beautiful beach, the houses, and green fields. How lovely it all was.

Papa told us to make haste and get dressed, for he was going onshore with a letter for Mr. G----[17], the great Madeira wine merchant, and would come back for us. He soon returned and took us onshore where we were all most kindly received by Mr. G. Who took us to his beautiful house where there was luncheon laid out, consisting of all sorts of nice things.

After that we went to see the lions. I don't remember much about the town, but we went to the nunnery

---

[17] Possibly this was Mr. Gordon, of Newton & Gordon Wine Merchants, a company which still exists today (in 2010) and which was active in Madeira in the early 19th century.

and the nuns came to the grating and talked to us, and showed their beautiful lace-work, feather flowers and a number of pretty things.

The grapes were hardly ripe, and instead of being in vineyards as we had been accustomed to see them in France, they were all beautifully trained.

It was managed that we should go next day to Mr. G's country house; so, early next morning there were palanquins, donkeys and ponies at the door to take us up. We had some rides to go. Boys were shouting and pulling the donkeys by their tails. It was all great fun and we had a delightful drive up.

When we arrived at the house it seemed a perfect paradise, and moving about the grass, delightful, after having been shut up in the ship for so long.

There was a beautiful lunch prepared for us, such delicious fruit and everything that you could think of. After spending a day there, never to be forgotten by us, we returned to Funchal rather tired and very sorry that we should have to return to the ship next morning, for the 'Princess Charlotte' was to sail at ten.

So there was an end to our pleasure, Mr. G sent us back loaded with everything he could think of, fruit of every kind, both fresh and preserved, and it was long before we came to an end of his kind presents.

How sorry we were to go onboard the dirty ship again, and how we used to talk of the happy time we spent at Madeira and it still occupies a very green spot in my recollection.

We had two months more of the ship, for after we left Madeira the weather was very fine. We were often becalmed, and they used to go out sometimes in a boat and bring in curious seaweed, etc. and the sunsets were most glorious.

It got very hot as we approached near the Line and, as we crossed it, we were told that Neptune would come on board and that he would shave any who had not crossed the Line before. So, accordingly one day there was a great commotion among the sailors, and in a short time there was a tremendous noise, shouting and welcoming on board. He hailed the ship and was received in great state. He was dressed up in seaweed and shells hung about him.

He called for shaving materials and bits of iron hoops and tar were brought, with which he set to work upon those who had crossed the line for the first time – unless they tipped the sailors. The shaving must have been rather a painful operation. It is never done now, and even in those days Neptune only went on board Merchantmen and Transports. It was not allowed on board men-of-war or John Company's ships. It was a piece of fun for the sailors and also for the passengers

– at least for those who were not too stingy to give to the sailors.

After Neptune's visit there was nothing more happened that was at all exciting except quarrels among the passengers who were beginning to get tired of one another having been so long shut up in the ship. Provisions were getting scarce, and the water nasty, as it was given out in small quantities, and we children used to be very thirsty, and were glad of the cold tea which was put by for us.

At last we drew near the cape, and the weather became very stormy again, as it always is in doubling the Cape.

The surf in Table Bay was tremendous, and the landing at Cape Town a serious business. We had to scramble down the side of the ship, and the boat going backwards and forwards and up and down, but the sailors caught us and at last we reached the quay in safety. But it was brown with cockroaches and we crunched them every step we took.

In those days there were no hotels at the Cape, only boarding-houses.

When we landed we went to see some gardens where there were refreshments of all kinds.

Papa left us there and went in search of a boarding-house. He was recommended one kept by a Dutch lady and her daughters; he took us there and we were most comfortable. There were several people there and a large party of us sat down to dinner. We were much amused by the little dark boys who stood behind us with large feather fans, flopping them about to keep off the flies.

The house appeared to be just under Table Mountain, which looked as if it were coming down upon us, but in reality it was a long way off. Beautiful flowers grew on Table Mountain, everlastings of the most beautiful colours. I believe there are wild animals there. We heard of a poor young officer having been killed up there by a tiger. The oranges at the Cape were very fine, so large and juicy and fresh gathered.

After we had been there two or three days at the Cape Papa was taken very ill and he was very anxious about all of us, but he remembered that he had a friend there, a Mr. Sheridan, the son of Richard Brinsley Sheridan[18]. He wrote to him and he came at once and was so kind, and used to come every day

---

[18] Richard Brinsley Sheridan, a playwright and author, was born in Dublin in 1751 and had two sons, Thomas Sheridan and Charles Brinsley Sheridan. It appears possible that the Mr. Sheridan referred to in the text is Thomas Sheridan.

and sit with Papa. They had much to talk about for they had not met for many years. Mr Sheridan held some civil appointment at the Cape[19].

Mrs Sheridan[20] was very kind and often used to come and take us out driving in her carriage, so in that way we saw something of the country. The hedges of myrtle and scarlet geranium were very beautiful, and one day she took us to the Government Gardens, where there were all sorts of beautiful shrubs and flowers, etc. splendid lions and tigers in cages, and a good many animals and birds going at large.

There were a great many monkeys among the trees.

Lord Charles Somerset[21] was the Governor, and there was to be a grand ball at Government House.

Mrs Sheridan asked my sister to go, with her, but Papa objected as they were in deep mourning. However

---

[19] Thomas Sheridan went to the Cape as Colonial Treasurer in 1813.
[20] Mrs Sheridan, nee Miss Cattendean, was reputed to be a lady possessed of great social gifts, considerable loveliness, and some intellect
[21] General Lord Charles Henry Somerset PC (2 December 1767 – 18 February 1831) was a British soldier, politician and colonial administrator. He was governor of the Cape Colony, South Africa, from 1814 to 1826.

Mrs Sheridan persuaded him, and there were dresses got for the occasion.

She asked if she might take me and said that she was going to take her own little girl, as it was going to be a very grand thing, and we might not have a chance of seeing anything like it again.

Miss Sheridan[22] was afterwards the Honourable Mrs Norton, a well known character, she was very pretty and so was her mother.

Of course, we were only lookers on, but I remember the gay scene. All Military and Naval officers in full dress, beautiful shrubs and flowers, all lighted up with coloured lamps, and the music very fine.

The outside was as brilliant as the inside; it was certainly a sight worth seeing.

If it had not been for the kindness of Mrs Sheridan, we should not have seen much of the Cape (town) for

---

[22] The Sheridans had three daughters: One became Duchess of Somerset; another became Lady Dufferin; and the third, certainly the most notorious, changed her name of Caroline Elizabeth Sarah Sheridan to the Hon. Mrs. George Norton when, aged nineteen, she married the Honourable George Norton, a twenty-seven year old barrister.

Papa never left his room till he went on board the transport which took us to St. Helena.

There were two transports that went regularly backwards to the Cape for provisions; for after Napoleon went there the population increased so much that there was not sufficient provision on the island[23]. The transport was very much crowded with animals of all kinds, we were much amused with the Cape sheep with their huge tails, in other respects they are like our own, but they looked thin and we were told that all the fat went into their tails.

---

[23] The 1817 census recorded 821 white inhabitants, a garrison of 820 men, 618 Chinese indentured labourers, 500 free blacks and 1,540 slaves.

St Helena

We were nearly three weeks on the passage to St. Helena when we arrived there on a beautiful morning and such a lovely blue sea, - but Oh! The dismal Rock! - where we expected to spend our lives. As Napoleon[24] said, "It was a brown rock bristling with cannons"[25].

We landed at a little quay, and walked along the shore until we came to some steps, at the top (of which) was a little gate which we went through, and then we were in James Town. The castle was on one side, the little church and churchyard on the other, and one long street.

There seemed to be but one shop, where all sorts of pretty things were sold. It belonged to a man of the name of Solomon, who also kept a boarding-house

---

[24] St Helena was chosen as the place of exile for Napoleon in 1815 and he was transported there in October of that year.
[25] Oliver Cromwell granted the East India Company a charter to govern the island of St. Helena in 1657 and the Company fortified the island in 1658.

and there we took up our abode, till something else turned up.

It was so dreadfully expensive that Papa said he could not afford to stay there, and as there was not a house to be got, the Governor, Sir Hudson Lowe[26], kindly said we might have rooms in the castle. So to the castle we went, and had a fine large room downstairs, and bedrooms and the use of the kitchens and a handsome room upstairs.

There was a fine terrace and commons pointing to the shore, a sentry-box, and sentries always walking up and down.

At the end of the terrace there was a footpath along the rocks, called 'the Lover's Walk'; nothing green there except the prickly pear which is all over the island.

For hours I used to sit on the Cannons watching the ships. There was a beautiful flagship, the

---

[26] Sir Hudson Lowe KCB, GCMG (28 July 1769 - 10 January 1844) was an Anglo-Irish soldier and colonial administrator who fought in the French revolutionary and Napoleonic wars. He received news of his appointment to the position of custodian of Napoleon Bonaparte and Governor of Saint Helena on the 1st of August 1815.

Northumberland[27], always stationary, and two ships of war, frigates always sailing round the island, one transport and several other small fishing boats, and often Chinamen and East-Indiamen anchoring at a distance for water. They were not allowed to come here and it was Papa's duty to go onboard every ship and inspect it when it anchored and when it went out, in case Napoleon should be carrying on any communication with it.

There was a signal-post at the castle and it was a great amusement watching the middies[28] making the signal. In this way passed some months of my childhood. A curious education for a small child (little girl); but a time that I look back upon with pleasure.

We used to watch the birds, the beautiful little avadavats[29], the large green canaries and turtle doves; these were the only birds belonging to the island.

The store where every kind of eatable was to be found was just below the castle, and I dare say that

---

[27] It is likely that this was the HMS Northumberland which had been the flagship of Rear-Admiral Alexander Cochrane in the Battle of San Domingo in 1806.
[28] A common term for midshipmen.
[29] Small weaver birds of the waxbill family (genus Amandava, family Estrildidae). The author identifies them as members of the finch family.

brought the birds, and also the rats, which were an enormous size and very numerous.

Our cats which we took there were the admiration of everybody, for the native cats were not much bigger than the rats. We used to hear the rats scampering and squeaking under our windows and were afraid that they would pay us a visit, but I suppose the smell of the cats kept them away.

There was no slavery, but there were old government slaves[30] who had charge of the castle and used to do our work. They were very nice old bodies. Most of the work on the Island was done by Chinamen[31], and they were very slow and terrible thieves. Opposite the room which we used as a sitting room was the Treasury – with a large iron book. One day when I was playing in the corridor some of the authorities asked me if I would like to see where the money was kept. I had always had a great wish to peep into that Blue Beard's closet, and now my time was come, and I

---

[30] The importation of slaves was made illegal in 1792 and Governor Lowe freed the remaining resident slaves in 1818.
[31] The East India Company imported Chinese labour to supplement the local workforce on the recommendation of Governor Robert Patton, who governed from 1802 to 1807.

went in and saw the bags of money, but I was terribly awe-stricken and glad to get out again.

The climate at St. Helena was very fine, not too warm, and never cold, but after the rainy season set in many people had dysentery, and most of our family had it pretty badly. Papa was the last to take it, he had eaten water-melon, and although his illness was caused by that, but he could not shake it off and he continued to get worse, and at last the doctor who attended him got alarmed about him.

Dr. Baxter[32], the physician to the forces, was a very clever man, and Papa had great confidence in him. At last poor Papa became very restless, and thought if he were moved into his own new house, he would get better, and Dr. Baxter said, "Let him have his way, it will do him no harm".

So Admiral Malcolm sent some of his sailors with a cot and he was carried in it, and he felt better, and was quite pleased with his house. There was a nice yard at the back, with a pond and some willow trees, and we had poultry there and we were all quite pleased, but poor papa got no better.

---

[32] Dr. Alexander Baxter, Deputy Inspector of Hospitals, was attached to the military garrison until 1820.

I had been promised to have a white frock and black sash on Easter Sunday, which was drawing very near.

Easter Sunday came on the 7th of April[33], and the white frock was put on in the morning, but there was no going to church.

Poor Papa was a great deal worse, and was wandering for the first time, and calling for paper, and ink, etc.

After church Lady Malcolm came in and said she would stay, and poor dear Papa got worse and worse, and in the evening, without much change, he breathed his last. We were all round the bed, and I, who was but a little girl, was rubbing his feet and saying how cold he was, but, Alas! It was the cold of death and in a short time we were orphans.

Lady Malcolm was very kind and let us indulge in our grief for some time before she gently took us away to her house which was close by. There she took us to our room and did everything for us.

It was not long before I had cried myself to sleep, but I knew that dear Papa was to be buried next day – for in that hot climate it was necessary that our dead should be buried out of our sight as soon as possible. So next morning early I saw my sisters get up and

---

[33] Captain Rainsford Hannay died in 1816 and Easter Sunday fell on the 14th that year.

dress themselves, and I was sure they were going to slip away without me.

I had always grieved so that I had never had a last look at Mama that I determined I would see Papa. So I put on my things and followed them, and saw dear Papa little changed looking peaceful and happy, all his cares at an end. Dear Papa who was always so kind to me, and took us everywhere with him, and now I should never see him again.

When we returned Lady Malcolm told us that Lady Howe wanted us to go up to Plantation House[34] and remain there till a homeward bound ship should arrive; but we must first get some black things, and that they would be made up at Plantation House.

While all our very kind friends were wondering what was to be done with us a whaler came in, and the Captain said he would remain a few days till we were ready to go. There was a nice woman at Plantation House who was waiting for a chance of going home and she was very glad to have charge of us, so just a week after poor Papa's death we left St Helena, and wretched we were to leave the Rock which had appeared so dreary to us a few months before;

---

[34] Plantation House, built in 1792, is still the residence of the governor of St Helena. It is located in the main street of James Town.

everything now appeared beautiful, and when it all was out of sight we lay down on the deck and felt as if our hearts would break.

My two eldest brothers remained behind, one with his regiment[35], and the other, who was almost fifteen[36], was taken by Sir Hudson Lowe as a sort of secretary and was to go on with his education.

---

[35] Major Frederick Rainsford Hannay of Kirkdale was born on 3 March 1810 and would have been six years old at the time of his father's death. It is likely that this reference is to the older brother who accompanied his father to France in 1802. Frederick Rainsford Hannay married Rhoda Johnston on 26 November 1840. He died on 21 January 1884 at age 73, with three daughters.

[36] William Henry Hannay was the son of Captain Thomas Rainford and Jane Hannay. He married Maria Dalrymple. He died in 1856, without issue. He may be the 'Uncle Bill' mentioned earlier in this memoir as the age would be approximately correct.

Return to England

The old Captain was a very kind man and did his utmost to make us as comfortable as he could, he gave us his own cabin, and had canvas put up to divide the sitting cabin and the one where our berths were. He came down every evening to play at cribbage with us, and he used to show us many curious things which he had brought from the Spice Islands.

We soon came in sight of the Island of Ascension, where we stopped for a short time for water and were very anxious to get on shore, but the Captain would not let us go. He said there was nothing to be seen but that he was only going to land to get some turtles and some plovers' eggs.

He brought four turtles on board, two were put into large tubs and the other two crawled about on deck and, in the course of time, were eaten when the fresh meat came to an end. They laid eggs on board; they were curious round things, and in course of time the little turtles came out, but they soon died.

We soon got into the trade winds, but nothing particular happened during the voyage, except a huge whale coming into view. The boats were lowered, and the sailors went after him, and harpooned him, and the sea was red with his blood, but he made his escape and the poor old Captain lamented over him exclaiming: "there she goes, look at her tail, see how she spouts!"

What a pity it was to be sure, he would have made a good thing by her if he had managed to get her.

We often met with curious birds and fishes.

England Again

One day the Captain announced that we should soon see England, but it was not very cheering to us, for the ship had been our home, and the rough kind old Captain our only friend.

At last we got into the river, and he told us that we must go on shore, for all sorts of people came on board and it would be no place for us to remain in; but where were we to go to?

We had no friends and there was no time to get an answer to a letter my sister had sent on shore informing our relations of our troubles, and our return to England; but the kind old Captain said he had some friends at Lime House who would be happy to have us and make us as comfortable as they could. So we were thankful to have some place to go to, and were so kindly received by a widow and her son and daughter, and never shall I forget their kindness; everything was so neat, and comfortable, and they did all they could for us.

We stayed with them for two or three days, and were very sorry when a hackney coach arrived and an old family butler to take us away.

At last we arrived with all our pets at a little lodging in Northumberland Street, a back street running out of Devonshire Street.

A cross-looking old woman received us at the door, and looked horrified when we all bundled out with our pets – two cats in a basket, a cage full of birds and a cockatoo, who immediately began to swear and, as his perch had been left on board he took possession of the back of a chair and began biting it to the dismay of the old woman, who seemed very much inclined to turn us all out. But two of our relations arrived and assured her that we should not be there long, for that some of us were going to school and the pets would be given away. This was not very pleasant intelligence to us and we all began to cry.

LIFE ALONE

I was the first to be packed off to school, and a wretched child I was, separated from my sisters and little brothers and everyone I cared for. I arrived at Ealing where I was kindly received by Madame Montfluery[37] and her daughters. It was the middle of the holidays so I did not see any of the girls for some time, and the daughters were very kind to me and put me up to many school ways.

When the girls arrived, of course, the new girl had much to put up with, and everything was so different to what I had been accustomed, but I sometimes thought y very heart would break and I used to sit in the corner by myself and cry.

---

[37] There were several girls schools in Ealing in the early 1800s which accepted a mix of boarders and day students. The St Mary's Road Girls Home for Destitute Children is also a possibility although it was in Acton at the time and moved to Ealing in 1867. There does not appear to be any reference to a Madame Montfluery and it is possible that this was an assumed name, that the author mis-remembered and/misspelt the name, or that she was a lower ranking teacher who did not rate a mention in the history books.

I was backward in my education and was put in a class with little girls much younger than myself, but I soon got above them and then I cheered up.

I was nearly a year at that school, for the Montfluery's recovered property in Normandy which they had lost at the time of the Revolution; so they gave up the school at Ealing and went to live there.

Then I went to a school at Rickmansworth and was very happy there for two years.

I was then invited to Scotland to stay with a cousin who lived near Edinburgh.

There were no steamers[38] in those days between London and Leith, so I came in a smack under charge of a Lady Anstruther[39], and we were ten days on board, and I was very sorry when we arrived at Leith, for I had been very happy and did not know what might be before me.

---

[38] The steamship 'James Watt' inaugurated the London to Leith service in 1821. The company still exists today as the General Steam Navigation Company under the ownership of P&O.
[39] Possibly a relation of Lady Janet Anstruther (nee Fall) for whom a 'bathing tower' was built circa 1750 near Elie, just north of Edinburgh. She died in 1802. The Anstruther family was quite prominent in the area at that time.

However, I was kindly received by my cousin, and after a few more wanderings I at last arrived at dear Kirkcudbright where I remained seven years and then married my first love.

The rest of my history you know, so I need say no more.

Looking back

I have had many sorrows and lost many who were dear to me, but I still have many left, and I have much reason to thank God for all the mercies he has vouchsafed to me.

Now I think I may finish off my recollections which should have been better.

Historical Notes

Frances Sophia McLellan neé Rainsford is listed in the 1841 Census living in the household of William Hannay McLellan. At the time of the census her age is given as 35, giving a birth year of 1806 (compared to approximately 1804 according to this memoir). Ages in the census were often rounded down, to the closest multiple of 5 so a person whose age is listed as 35 should have been between 35 and 40 years eleven months which would have given a birth year of between 1801 and 1806.

The memoir is quite definite that the author 'made her appearance' after war broke out in 1803.

The 1841 census records Frances' place of birth as 'British Subject, France'. The 1871 census records the place of birth as Bedale, Sabgar, France in 1806.

William Hannay[40] McLellan, Frances' 'first love' and husband, is the head of the household in 1841 and was born in 1806. He and Frances had four children[41]

---

[40] This name is variously spelt as Hanna, Hannah and Hannay in different references.

[41] Jane McLellan (aged seven and possibly named after her aunt Jane Rainsford), David McLellan (aged six), William McLellan (aged three) and Samuel McLellan (aged 1).

at the time of the census in 1841. Subsequent records indicate that they had six children in total[42].

Jane Rainsford, aged 40 in 1841, is also listed as resident in the household at the time of that census. It is possible that she is one of the 'two eldest brothers and sisters' that was taken to France with Thomas Rainsford and his son in 1802, before Frances was born. There is no record that Frances ever was reunited with her sisters and brothers after the end of the narrative. The Rainsford family was large, and well represented in the local area, so this name may just be a coincidence.

William McLellan, born in 1838, was a son of William Hannay and Frances Sophia McLellan. In the 1871 census he is shown as the oldest man in the household; his mother, Frances Sophia, is listed as the head of the household.

William subsequently married Janet G. McLellan (born 1853) and the couple is listed in the 1881 and 1891 censuses as residents of Kirkcudbright. They had several children[43] one of whom, Jane, had the original

---

[42] Jane (born 1834), David (born 1835), William (born 1838), Samuel (born 1840), Thomas Ramesfield or Rainsford (born 1842), and Sophia Mary (born 1851).
[43] Frances R McLellan (born 1876), William H McLellan (born 1877), Frederick R H McLellan (born 1880), Jane F McLellan (also known as Jean; born 1882 and

manuscript of this book; another child, Frederick, became the father of Andrew John Lines McLellan[44].

As Jane died childless her transcription of manuscript found its way into the possession of her nephew, Andrew. That transcription was inherited by David Aksel Hannay McLellan.

It has now been published in this form by his wife, Julie, and will be inherited by his son, Andrew James.

---

possibly named after her great aunt and/or aunt) and Loftus P McLellan (born 1884).

[44] Andrew John Lines McLellan, born 1924, died 1995.